WOMEN
TRAVELING
ALONE

PUBLISHED BY AVOCET BOOKS
www.avocetbooks.com

ISBN:
Paperback   979-8-9890381-4-5

First Edition

BOOK PRODUCTION BY HAL CLIFFORD ASSOCIATES
www.hcabooks.com

Women Traveling Alone

poems

Marte
Carlock-Clifford

Dedicated to
all women traveling alone

Contents

I.

Women Traveling Alone	3
Climbing to Cruising Altitude	4
First Evening in Kyoto	5
In a Six-tatami Room	6
At Toksugung	7
Haiku for Rajasthan	8
Dawn at the Taj	8
In a Red Sari	9
Daughters	10
On the Andaman Sea	11
Out of Seoul	12
Altostratus	13
Over South Dakota	14
Between Flights at Dade	15
Changing Planes at Miami	16
Hotel Maid	17
Raven	18
The Voice of the Tinamou	19
In Carib Waters	20
Acieques	21
Antigua	22
Surin Reef	23
Silverton	24
Lines from the Sneffels Wilderness	25
On Mount Flume	26
White Dot Trail	27
Fragments from Alaska	28
Incident at Aspen	29
Haiku for the Baggage Carousel	30
Geography at Point Reyes	31

II.

Old Bridle Path, Mount Lafayette 35

Vintage Photograph 36

Hutwoman 38

Sun Dog 39

Descending Carrigain 40

Bug Season 42

Haiku for the Front Range 43

Day Moon 43

On Interstate 84, Windchill Minus 40 44

While Driving 45

The Landscape of Dreams 46

The Bluebird Lady 47

Kingfisher 48

Dandelions 49

Coyote 50

Perched 51

The Trophy Wife 52

The Poison Ivy Tree 53

Luncheon 54

Expectation 55

Machines 56

Old Houses Talk 57

Digging Out Daylilies 58

Baby Oak 59

Black Cherry 60

Before the Storm 61

Skiing at Margy's Hut 62

Haiku for December 63

Haiku for the Chipmunk 64

Haiku for March 65

Leafout 66

From Doublet Hill 67

Haiku for Early June 68

Petals 69

Sugar Season 70

Rubythroat 71

Drought Season 72

Haiku After a Rainstorm 73

III.

Artemis 77

Eden 78

On Your Birthday 79

Night 80

Ghostin' 81

Sleeping in My Granddaughter's Room 82

On Hearing the Famous Feminist Poet 83

Waiting 84

Familiar Face 85

Pink Helmet 86

Treasure 87

Gem of the Garden 88

I Used to Dream 89

On Reading Emily Dickinson 90

The Daughter She Wanted 91

Key 92

Racquets Court 93

Puritan Ethic 94

Calendar 95

Birthday Party 96

Bighat People 97

Sisyphus 98

Finish Line 99

Veteran 100

Psychic Powers 101

Could 102

Before Drinking Hemlock 103

Stand Ready 104

Acknowledgments 106

About the Author 107

I.

WOMEN TRAVELING ALONE

In the ladies' room
   we almost collide
sorry   sorry

in that half-second glance we recognize ourselves
   drably dressed
   crophaired bespectacled flatshod
   towing tiny practical carry-ons

competent
unhurried
unafraid yet

a little bit unsure what sort
   of welcome we'll receive.

CLIMBING TO CRUISING ALTITUDE

For a while we must fly blind
  fog a surgical bandage on the windshield's eye

this cloud could hold death
  another blind craft
                  erring

we cannot think of that
  we have followed procedures
             checklists, rules
  all the flight plan specifies

we know we are right
there's no choice but to fly on
          trusting

FIRST EVENING IN KYOTO

Up the downsloped steps
     of Kiyomizu temple
  her father
  my son
carries her on his back

bright as her eyes
   its seven-tiered tower is orange, blue
      glarelighted against the dusk

we buy a luck charm
take a longhandled dipper from
 violetsterile glow
 sip from the cascade
      descend and wander among shopstalls
        past paper houses
        dark temples

      under a dragon roof we sit
in shadows
her mother feeds her

On his back she sleeps
    when we walk on.

IN A SIX-TATAMI ROOM

Fragile as a kite
   the door slides aside
                          outside
   an empty pair of clogs waits
in them my eye walks
stone to stone into moss

from bamboo spout
               drop by drop
  water fills a basin
     shallow-gouged from rock

dipper waits
blossom waits
berry waits

pine branch is a stain
   against a fence of bamboo
   split and bound

in the night I hear rain
I contemplate the shape of wood
   framing paper white as rice.

AT TOKSUGUNG

The great hall of the king
    bears a dragon roof
            tile stacked on iron-hued tile
high as a dragon's spine

beams and columns underside
    are paintbox bright
            green blue carmine
            dragonscale gold

dragons twine at roofpeak

where the monarch sits
    red sun at his left
    yellow for his queen

the five green mountains bless
            health
            wealth
            long life
            good spouse
            easy death

five traditional blessings for the kings of Korea

scuffing yellow gingko leaves
    I descend the steps pondering what's missing
            the greatest blessing
                    strong daughters
                    wise sons.

HAIKU FOR RAJASTHAN

In India they build
    temples on the peaks of hills
knowing mountains are holy.

DAWN AT THE TAJ

A falcon lives in one of the minarets
    she has a kill this morning
            tears at something I cannot see from here
in the dew mynahs, busy, converse rudely
green parakeets are arrows

the marble looks blue
    finally the onion dome begins to glow
            creamy
on the side where the sun is rising.

IN A RED SARI

In a red sari she leaves the well
   balancing a column of copper pots on her head
      three for her
      two for her daughter
she squats in the dust of her doorstep
   proud of rings and bangles
   talking with her friend
   feet planted flat

holding her son
   she draws her sari across her face
   across the baby too
      her only acknowledgment of my presence
I am a face on a passing bus
   a phantom from another time.

DAUGHTERS

The guide is petite, gamine, speaks five languages
       good enough English with a charming accent
At lunch she discovers you speak Spanish and converses with you
       in Spanish saying she needs practice as do you
She confides she is getting married in September she wonders where
       you would suggest they go for a honeymoon
You think of her as a daughter, as a friend
       when the tour of Budapest is over
           you invite her to visit you in Cleveland you part with tears

In the next city the guide is petite, blond,
       pretty in a Slavic sort of way she has a nice smile, speaks good
       English with a charming accent
on the carriage ride she shares the carriage with you, you ask her about her
children, her husband, you start thinking of her as a daughter

ON THE ANDAMAN SEA

A paradise in theory
   bleached beach reaching for the curve of earth
trade winds swelling tepid seas
beak-burdened hornbills lumbering from tree to tree

We sit on driftwood benches
   to critique each night's sunset

   heaven on earth

still I can't help wanting to be
where I know the voices of the birds.

OUT OF SEOUL

Below us plumgray cloud seas
       exhale dragon breath
on dragon wings we rise
    to meet the night
       gobbling up a time zone every hour

the polestar rises with us
    its wheel of constellations arrayed
    in plan I cannot see at home

To cross such seas Magellan labored a hundred days

we will arrive
      in theory
    before we left.

ALTOSTRATUS

All day the blue was flawless
   but at twilight the sky
   became pleated and corduroyed
like beach sand in the shallows
where the water foams and
      shyly withdraws.

OVER SOUTH DAKOTA

Rumpled like an unmade bed
      the earth below is marked with a rusty seam
   through the valley and over a pass
     empty
     dusty

but somebody's road home.

BETWEEN FLIGHTS AT DADE

Moonfaced, overweight and doesn't care
   carries a briefcase not a backpack
   certainly not a wheeled carry-on
but wears a college sweatshirt
Asian perhaps but something says
      I was born here
She doesn't try to talk to the woman sitting at her elbow
   who is after all with a man
I finish my chili, my g&t, try to flag down the harried waitress
The roundfaced woman catches my eye and shrugs
   we smile
I have time I say and settle back
   later I wave bill and credit card in the air
   the waitress swoops in and takes them

The woman does a double thumbs up
We could have been friends.

CHANGING PLANES AT MIAMI

Surely her man will join her any minute
 women like this don't travel alone
streaked hair kohled eyes Vuitton luggage
she doesn't order food
 just twirls her glass of grigio sips genteelly
looks like so many other women I want to say Peggy
what are you doing here
but Peggy may have let herself go gray by now

I can watch the basketball game playing above the bar
 She stares into space
   props one foot on her Vuitton
   it's a sneaker, says Rocket Dog on the sole
    not what you'd expect
I'd like to sit across from her
 talk and see if we have anything in common
eating alone is terrible, drinking alone more so

Who knows, she might like company
 but she does not see me at all.

HOTEL MAID

You never see her but
   you know she's been here
tail of the toilet paper origamied
   into a triangle, or knotted like a full-blown rose
pillows plumped and bed turned down
mints—two even though I am only one
       (I tuck them into my bag for later
        who wants chocolate at bedtime?)

I am careful to hang up my towel responsibly
   to indicate another use
to coathanger my clothes out of sight, put the toiletries
   back in their case and off the sink
align my shoes in the closet
hide my book and flashlight in the drawer

I try to make the room look like it's being used by a nice person

In return she fails to vacuum
I spend three days looking at the same dust ball
     under the bed.

RAVEN

Atop the drainpipe
    at an angle of the Roman wall she
sits on a careless twigpile so still
    I'm sure she is fake
then she blinks, gives her feathers a shake

Always there, dark and sun, impervious
    to rain never heard of boredom
never seems to eat
    does she ask where her mate has gone
what other bird he's claimed

I will leave long before she does.
    in my brain she will sit always there

doing what the universe ordains.

THE VOICE OF THE TINAMOU

Great tinamou's voice fills up the dusk
   long oboe notes linked
       breathe in
breathe out

this from a bird we never see
   it echoes our own breath for the rest of time
breathe in
      breathe out

the sound of the jungle
     meditating

IN CARIB WATERS

The boat writes through the seas
       like the finger of God
   creating worlds in its wake

volcanoes rise and erupt
      spew white magma
  lava the color of ice
galaxies spin out of froth
      spitting constellations that
  hang a second on the wind

         collapse
and cease to be.

ACIEQUES

The island recedes astern
       like a bad idea
   discarded but
lingering on the horizon of the mind

it emerges now and then from haze
    to tempt and tantalize

ANTIGUA

Leashed to the moon
    the tread of surf walking the seabed
  scrubs our brains

Birds spurn the crumbs of converse
    leaving them to shrivel in narcotic air

Hot winds blow through this place
    sucking ambition from our bodies
  like dust vacuumed up

We lose cognizance
    succumb to ancient mesmerisms, to
  the tick and tock of planetary blood

We sleep like stones

My eyes go blank in the glare. It
    erases our thoughts like beachprints
  scours the meat from our hollows and
throws us empty on the sand.

SURIN REEF

Frozen clouds
        calcified fireworks
  bluetipped
explode on the sea floor

Bitesized iridescent rainbows
    swim without fear toward my mask

In a plume of bubbles
    his hands white as a dead man's
  my son sinks toward the reef
        flicks calmly like a huge parrotfish

so long that
    I am afraid for him
        then
   he rises to the air.

SILVERTON

Miner's handlebar mustache
  uninterested eyes
    not much grammar in his speech
the jeep rental man moves deliberately
    rebuke to us who come from efficient lives

I wait outside
  zipped against the sky

Across the road a hill rises
  in paintbox colors
  crusted with sedimentary rock

for one instant I remember how it was
  before I lived so long
  walked so many mountains
  saw so much

when the world stood fresh
  portent of all I had yet to see
      of many paths, many choices, many lives
      open, still unchosen
for an instant.

Then the jeep man gives us the keys and
  we travel into the known world.

LINES FROM THE SNEFFELS WILDERNESS

1.

Lupine that chooses to grow in the trail
is crushed by the horse's hoof.

2.

Long before autumn
geranium puts out one red leaf
practicing.

3.

Resin and faint refrigeration
perfume the ponderosa grove
jays and flickers chide.

4.

Freckled fritillaries gather
where the horses shat
mice have eaten the thumb
off a wrangler's lost glove.

5.

Ski runs scar the ridge's palm
read its future in those lines
if you can.

ON MOUNT FLUME

Where the Osseo trail begins to climb
a runner passes us in silence
    barebacked
    loping lightly from rock to root
    his shirt flapping from his waistband

we are laden with knapsacks
        water, food, jackets
     bandages
     emergency gear

He carries nothing
there will be no
   storm mishap heat hunger thirst
       that his will cannot overcome.

He will run to Greenleaf and back today

he is young
he believes he is a god.

WHITE DOT TRAIL

Yellow hard hat
   wispy red beard
  the trail builder pries at a rock

he has laid a peeled pine water bar
   a garish backslash
  across this trail wide as a city street

there are others and
  a rivulet behind every one

there is no green on the trail
     just
  boulders bedded in mud
   not even forest duff

where we step
        nothing grows.

FRAGMENTS FROM ALASKA

Raindrops make stars on spruce water
I paddle into tidal grass
    the sea lifts my boat over
    a trail that sucked my boots off
        an hour before

Kayaks like salmon hover, schooled
    a face pops out of the current
        looks us over
        slaps water and is gone.

INCIDENT AT ASPEN

Routinely
   he puts the icy north faces below him
   lifts red slopes
      tufts of juniper and rabbitbrush
   zeroes in on the chip of airstrip
   kisses the wheels
   touches the brakes

there are no brakes
            no flaps

He cannot steer
   coolly hits switches
   the man at his side following
      cool
      frantic

the aircraft a loose cannon on a gun deck
   careening toward its loaded twin
      waiting on a side strip
   its passengers witness disaster roaring at them
      tires exploding
      smashing runway markers
it comes to rest
      in a snowbank

Holy shit
   he says

In a rearmost seat I sit
      amazed
      alive
      reborn
into a new age
         old age
where nothing can be taken for granted.

HAIKU FOR THE BAGGAGE CAROUSEL

Slow as years our bags
   cycle by. The right one may
or may not appear.

GEOGRAPHY AT POINT REYES

A generation and a continent ago
        I remember you small against the sun
your hair fair as California grass

Now satyr bearded
        backpack burdened
you walk ahead

Beyond this ridge the ocean expands
        blue and boundless as your future
behind me lies North America
        knotted and convoluted
   as my journey home.

II.

OLD BRIDLE PATH, MOUNT LAFAYETTE

For us it is an easy trail
yet I think of the horses when this path was new
   unbalanced by long-skirted riders
      sideways in the saddle
little shrieks and exclamations
   as their mounts extend their necks
   lunge up the slab
hooves clumsy, stumble on root
strike rock, dislodge stones
   to bounce downward, threatening fetlocks
      silencing warblers

the guide has built a lodge for his clients
will give them a supper of beef and beans

the horses, watered at a mucky tarn
penned in the stone corral that still exists
   pass the night in high fog.

VINTAGE PHOTOGRAPH

Stirrup to stirrup the riders line up
   eighteen young women attired alike
   white shirts with sailor ties
   berets probably red, all sepia now

Girls giggling, horses all bay, all alike
   their phalanx flanked by two hatless men
   fair-haired, impeccable, on larger horses
then at the end a few children on ponies, donkeys
summer sun makes them squint

The photographer huddles under his black hood
   his work becomes an heirloom
   a meter long and half a foot high

Daughters of privilege
   they will become flappers, then wives, then divorcées
   women left behind by war
    will turn their children over to nannies
   their houses to hired women
   will die of lung cancer and alcohol

The photo will travel wall to wall
   until nobody knows what to do with it
nor which rider became great-grandmother

The horses are restive, inattentive
one rider, chatting, fails to keep hers in place
for the perfect shot

Never imagining how much trouble it will be
   a century later
   to box and ship such an object
to her great-granddaughter, also a rider
   and already older than she was then.

HUTWOMAN

Had I been born forty years later
   long-legged and strong
I would have grown a tawny blond braid
   worn brown bib overalls over a white leotard
carried great loads lightly
   been friends with bearded hutmen
   lover of none
run up boulder fields
   passing knee-braced hikers with a smile
gloried in my mastery of heights and distances

Focused on this sharp path
   I think I am alone until
bootscrape on rock tells me
   she's at my shoulder
I step aside
she thanks me and with a jeté she is gone
   sure she will never be so old
         so slow

SUN DOG

Descending to aspen I halt
   to see late green light
       streaming
through pale green tree trunks
       like a sunshot underwater world

just above the ridge a rim of cirrus
      prisms the spectrum
   to a broad combat ribbon
         huge and brilliant

I reach the hellebore swamp
      my sunglow has shrunk to a pink flag

when I emerge in a flowered meadow
      it is gone.

DESCENDING CARRIGAIN

Much too soon
  I've started listening for the river

the woods are so silent I think I've gone deaf
  soft scuff of boot
  duff-touch of trekking pole
          my pulse

  but no bird
  no breeze
    descending hikers past me long since

  moosewood singed by drought
  birches, starving,
    their early-shed leaves littering the path

dry gullies at my left
  I step off-trail to peer into them
                no river

finally I cross a whisper of slow water
hours later
  I hear it
    music
    life
increasing

at the final crossing
  people have erected monuments
    river stones balanced on end

menhirs with lintels atop
art
magic

I stand midstream in awe
blessed.

BUG SEASON

Mouth closed so I don't ingest blackflies I labor
   upward through the woods
they fail to find me until I break a sweat
    then they are infinite
    seeking the pools of my eyes

At the lookout, breeze and a respite, then
   all the way down I am a fountain, an oasis, a flower
they pursue and confront me
   a dizzy happy dance before my eyes
ravenous for me the feast

If I hurry, in ten minutes I'll be behind screens
   on a day like this a contender for
the greatest invention of civilization.

HAIKU FOR THE FRONT RANGE

Spectral acrobat
    balled tumbleweed somersaults
over the pale grass.

DAY MOON

White day moon lies
    on its back like a puppy
who wants its belly scratched.

ON INTERSTATE 84, WINDCHILL MINUS 40

Snow ghosts
   still looking for someone

rise up out of the gullies

      walk beside the car
      throw gravel
      peer in the windows

        shake us
            asking
            asking

WHILE DRIVING

I used to write poems while driving
    tedium of asphalt
        unreeling
    lulling rhythms of good shock absorbers
released doves of metaphor
        songbirds
        thrushes

I haven't written poems for a long time
I see many more hawks than I used to.

THE LANDSCAPE OF DREAMS

Sometimes I am in a familiar house
    my grandmother's I think
   and I find stairways and rooms I never knew were there
    I never get to explore them

Sometimes I am traveling but there are difficulties
    I never arrive

Sometimes I fly
   the land unscrolling far below me
    never long enough yet

    I don't remember landing

THE BLUEBIRD LADY

Bold song, the house wren's,
   arpeggios fortissimo, much finer
      than the vacillating converse
      of the blue thrush

The bluebird lady shoos away wrens
   but kills sparrows
   tosses their nests out
      of her bluebird boxes, and if
she catches a sparrow she wraps it in a cloth
hits it with a hammer
   and tosses it to her cat

Never knew she would do such a thing but
   sparrows kill bluebirds
and fair's fair.

KINGFISHER

Uniformed like a bandsman
  stiffpeaked hat
  cadetgray coat
  bandoliered in buff
she sounds warning tattoos
  on her treble snare drum

a Napoleonic figure
  bigheaded arrogant short
     she chooses a high reviewing stand
     to assess the world

on the river corrugations
  break the sky
into impressionistic strokes

she is not distracted
  her gaze pierces all

    rising

she hangs in the air
an avenging angel weighing fates
     unerring, strikes.

DANDELIONS

Tooth of lion, fierce name
  for such an innocuous little flower

How can a man not like it
  scattered smiling in the grass?
But no
  he wants no weeds
  and it must be one
      because no one plants it

Dig them out. He wants grass
      pure and boring.

COYOTE

She trots up the trail toward my window
   tawnyblack German shepherd
whose dog is that I think
      running loose
   contrary to municipal code

sensing my gaze she lifts her muzzle
   a hunter's muzzle, pointed
  longer than any dog's

Git, I say
      she vanishes into the woods

sometimes I see her again
     following the stream
      purposeful
      hunting
     never coming near the house.

PERCHED

How does she know I'm not a danger
    scoping her with binoculars
when it could be a rifle

color of treebark
    she sits impassive, maybe digesting

I wish she would catch the mouse
    that makes a home in my garage

How does the mouse know
    she's safe in the garage
        and in mortal danger under the sky

We want to be the hawk, fearless
    not the scurrying neurotic mouse
        how much better if we all were horses
            running free
            eating grass.

THE TROPHY WIFE

The trophy wife
    yellow hair upflipped below her ears
swings her sport utility vehicle
    (big as a bus)
out of the driveway of the turreted trophy house
    (big as a castle)
onto what was once a country lane

She meets a rival vehicle, a mirror of her own
    they cannot pass
she shifts (automatic stick on the floor, 4WD 380 horse)
    into reverse and backs into her driveway again

Fucking inconvenient, she thinks

She digs into her bag for her smartphone
    (small as a pack of cards)
    and punches a key

Honey? Couldn't you call this hick town
    and make them do something about this stupid little road?
She taps the red button, considers it done.

Across the road the paint, the bay, the Appaloosa stand
    (in the only farmyard left)
    mute and unopinionated

How nice to see horses, she thinks
How scenic.

THE POISON IVY TREE

She never meant to entertain such a guest
        much less marry it
but it got a fingerhold when she wasn't looking
busy pumping sap and putting out leaf
   before she knew it
she found herself embraced
       hidden behind poison ivy leaves
entangled in vines that extend impudent branches
       alienating passersby
         pretending it does so on her behalf.

LUNCHEON

They gather, hug, sit, lay sunglasses on the table
   shake out napkins
a little shy
they haven't been together for a long time
one can hardly walk now, one has endured
   the poisons of therapy
one has a son who is a crack addict
   they don't ask about him
another has a titanium hip, a mechanical knee
two live alone, they are content, but
   their children worry
they eat, talk, make jokes about their lives
   finally stand and hug again realizing how much
after so many years
they value one another.

EXPECTATION

The grandmother I didn't like was stout and deaf
   paid no attention to children, wore a flat black hat to church
My mother made us go. I only remember
   the fans in the pewback
   circles of cardboard printed with Bible verses
      glued to a stick
Grandmother grew figs and hydrangeas
   I've never liked either one

Bored, my brother and I would walk after dinner to the grade
crossing
   hunker by the track to watch the Zephyr go by.
As the dusk grew we would wait
               wait, infinitely wait
finally with a thrill we would see the headlight far off
   it seemed not to move
      not to grow larger
still we waited, losing patience

Suddenly the light was huge over our heads
      a blast of sound and air
      blurred past us and was gone
leaving us crouched
        disappointed
  in the weeds.

MACHINES

Wheeling down into the parking lot
I'm met by a boy on a motor bike
        accelerating
    his buddies stand helmets in hand, grinning
he finds glee in unmuffled combustion
draws rubber circles on the macadam

I swerve to one side looking
    for some safe way through
    to the bike trail narrow between goldenrods

we look but don't greet one another
      wary
      each pitying the other

they are young, they are men
      and in love with machinery.

OLD HOUSES TALK

Old houses talk to you
       this one talks to me at least
  I'm not fluent in its language
  geriatric complaints and creaks
      but I get the gist of it and I sympathize

I didn't like the house at first
too ordinary although
  it came with a forest out the back door and gardens at its feet

we have grown into each other
  it is sleeker
  I am more ordinary
     now
  I wouldn't leave it for anything.

DIGGING OUT DAYLILIES

This is an old garden now
we pull out more than we plant

sometimes I find an overgrown yew bush
        in a corner of the woods that
   must have been a planting bed when
Mrs. Bartolini put it there

It makes me think of how this acre might have looked
        when the house was new
on barescraped land begging for something green

she with all this space to plant as she pleased
coming out in the morning, cultivating her salvia

and the mister, coming home at night
   unreeling the hose and watering everything
before he even changed his shoes.

BABY OAK

Baby oak clings to its leaves all winter
      like a toddler hoarding his toys
  yet to learn
there'll be more and better leaves
      as life goes on.

BLACK CHERRY

Arthritic and frail
   its bones break at any storm's touch
   one limb hanging by a tendon
blooms anyway

   a drop of burgundy at every heart
   petals bluepink
   pale as the moon of my fingernail

It has scions
   a grove all blooming
   growing up undisciplined, untended

my garden needs a cherry but
     this is not my land
I don't dare take even one.

BEFORE THE STORM

Snowflake motes linger in the air
      like idlers waiting for a mob to form
unspoken ideas
too insubstantial to fall

little flakes, big snow, the old-timers say
  I oil the shovel, wait for them to grow.

SKIING AT MARGY'S HUT

Williams Ridge is a layered
    chocolate torte
        its sky cream
        earth sugar

sweet the sound of patterns we carve
down the burn
    and into elegant spruce.

HAIKU FOR DECEMBER

A great pruning wind
  in the night clipped the digits
of my winter pines.

HAIKU FOR THE CHIPMUNK

Lord of the forest
    red-tail screams, predicts misfortune
for all prey species.

HAIKU FOR MARCH

Windblown robins, still
   silent but jays bugle through
the lengthening day.

LEAFOUT

All winter I could see across the brook
    into the heart of the woods
suddenly the forest draws a veil and hides
        as it changes into summer clothes.

FROM DOUBLET HILL

In morning glare the
  tin cutout skyline sits like
a backdrop for a stage.

HAIKU FOR EARLY JUNE

Wood thrush at sunset
  a Tibetan singing bowl
  rings
through my bones.

PETALS

Magnolia petals
   like yesterday's socks
litter the rug of new grass.

SUGAR SEASON

She has no lovers now
   a husband, yes
   children, yes

empty receptacles all
tapping her arteries
      she is a maple tree standing in snow
      hung with scores of buckets
one more might kill the tree yet
   they hang it

and she goes on producing
      bud, leaf, clear juices
   they drain it and take it away

She wonders whether
      she will ever blossom again.

RUBYTHROAT

A drab bird
      (only he wears the jewel)
feeds on cardinal flower
probing every tube on the stalk
      quick and efficient

You might mistake her for an insect

Her sister swooping drives her off
then shuns the crimson flowers
samples silverbell instead and is gone

Insouciant she appears again
stabs each red tube
never the same one twice
      efficient and quick.

DROUGHT SEASON

Outside, the world turned gray
       a scrim over the trees
so long since we had rain I could not
    think what it was

I went to stand at the glass door to watch
       as the miracle of water
yet not water but hail
began to collect on the deck

you and I stood shoulder to shoulder
    feasting on summer snow.

HAIKU AFTER A RAINSTORM

Thunder scrubs soiled clouds
    on a washboard sky to wring
out the final drops.

.

III.

ARTEMIS

For centuries she was a goddess
       a timekeeper
       an omen
       a song
now human footprints mar her face
   we know her secrets
       her plains and mountains
       her deserts
       her dust
       her thirst
still she can rise pink and handsome
       after that she just keeps us awake
   insisting it's day.

EDEN

In truth there was never a snake or an apple
        and they knew already about lust, had known forever
        what creature didn't

It was that they lived long
        saw the wolf and the tiger grow old and die
        saw the tree fern and gingko wither and fall
        saw even the snake
        become food for vultures

It wasn't sex they discovered
it wasn't the knowledge of good and evil

they discovered death and
        terrified, they invented God

ON YOUR BIRTHDAY

Congratulations
   although we have it all wrong
you made the leap from amniotic sea
 and became an air-breathing creature and all
 not on your own initiative

It's not about you, really

Congratulate your mother
   a year almost of self-denial
   then pain and rupture
   then your demands for decades

Yes, happy birthday, human, but
  celebrate that woman.

NIGHT

I loved the night as it used to be
        lush with stars
but here cityglow erases sky
I lie wakeful listening to the night
        then fall asleep when it's day

Is this how it will happen
that night becomes my day and day the night
        until I can't tell the difference anymore.

GHOSTIN'

My father slept the sleep of the self-righteous
    snoring great decibels
while my mother prowled the little house
    dark kitchen, empty bedroom that once was mine,
    living room with the rug she hooked from scraps
sleepless
ghostin' around, he called it.

Fifty years on in a different house
I do the same sometimes, ghostin'
    but I have an antidote
    hot milk with a shot of rum

She would be aghast and I would believe her except
    in her middle years I found a fifth
    of sweet Manischewitz tucked
in the back corner of her closet

her secret antidote I guess for a life that wasn't
    the one she wanted.

SLEEPING IN MY GRANDDAUGHTER'S ROOM

Years ago a child
pasted a cardboard star
   to the ceiling above her bed.

She doesn't live here anymore

the star has been painted over
   yet in the dark
you can still see the glow.

ON HEARING THE FAMOUS FEMINIST POET

It's not her fault she's only one inch tall
    the college chapel is huge and crowded
so many of us wanting so much from her

nor that she has grown old
    with any luck who doesn't

But she reads us trifling poems about her little dog
          no soaring nature lyrics
     no sidesaddle allusions to love
         no summer and seafroth

just her dog, an old woman's infatuation

WAITING

Outside the medical office
   there is a bench thank god
      carefully she sits and waits

it was nice of that woman to volunteer
   to bring her here but now she waits
   she had to wait in the doctor's office of course
      it seems she has to wait everywhere now
as if they think her time is worthless

How could it be
   when there's so little of it
            left.

FAMILIAR FACE

I should know your name but
     a lot of people have walked through the gates of memory

Some stroll a bit
  some plant a flower
  some prune a tree or cut it down
sometimes I give someone a seedling to take away

Some pitch a tent and camp whether I want them to or not

Most walk in, look around and go out again

 So no, I'm sorry
  tell me who you are.

PINK HELMET

Pink helmet, pink scooter, pink tutu, pink sneakers
      she glides through a forest of legs, a hundred legs
  in front of the hot dog stand
not caring where her parents are

TREASURE

Misers count their pennies
         one by one
kings fling coins to the populace
    the forest divests its gold every annum

for us a winter evening is impoverished
    but as recompense
caught in a naked tree there's a planet
        masquerading as a diamond.

GEM OF THE GARDEN

Jewelweed just doesn't care
    muscles its way up through mulch, vines, grass
its bloom a topaz gem fit for a delicate finger
belying its true persona
    rude, jostling, taking charge of everything

Each jewel begets hundreds

We remember its first name, jewel
        forgetting its patronymic, weed.

I USED TO DREAM

I used to dream of mountains
    summits blessed by ravens
    meadows full of grass
        of paths of love leading
    through valleys sweet with fern

These days boulders underlie my bed
    I celebrate false summits
    descend to canyons clogged with ice
infinite crevasses split the glacier
    somewhere above
        an avalanche sounds.

ON READING EMILY DICKINSON

Correspondence a double pleasure
first the joy of words from friends
   whose faces she refused to see

then the paper
   steaming the envelopes flat
   fitting her words to their shapes
diamonds, parallelograms
   hasty scrawls in soft pencil

      so hard to read

Mabel deciphered, broke the code
   gave us the poems
   the masterworks

I type my writing, pretty sure
   there are no Mabels anymore.

THE DAUGHTER SHE WANTED

I was not the daughter she wanted
  she was not the mother I needed
Much later when I was a parent myself
  she called to say I'm sorry I
    wasn't a better mother

I wanted to say
  What brought this on

we had never had heart-to-heart talks
  instead I said oh mother
  nobody knows how
    to do this
We all just do the best we can

It never occurred to me to say I love you anyway

I never heard the word love in that house
  Jesus loves you the song said
    your parents maybe not so much.

KEY

A year ago it was a precious thing
   a treasure, guarded
it opened magic rooms and vistas
   of lake, of geese and ospreys

then the locks were changed
   gleaming as ever, promising as ever
   this key has no more value
than a tin can

it's hard to throw a key away
it was once so prized

some day I'll find it again
hold it in my hand and wonder
   what mystery it unlocked.

RACQUETS COURT

This game
  how can it be a poem
      absent nobility
      absent insight
          emotions
          aspirations
only small goals
  met unmet
      soon forgotten
only banter
      friends
      sun
      wind
      bright trees
all the same
  on my deathbed it will be
  among my best memories.

PURITAN ETHIC

Prodded by the Puritan ethic,
    Mrs. Roosevelt asked herself each evening
What have you done today that is worthwhile?

She was a little older than Eleanor Roosevelt, my grandmother
    but I doubt she ever asked herself
    whether she had done anything that day
that was worthwhile

paid the leather-shouldered iceman
    who came with fifty pounds on his back
        (never had a refrigerator)
walked to the grocery store and back with her paper bags
        (never learned to drive)
roasted chickens in case her kin came to see her
made the bed, did the laundry
went to church
did whatever had to be done on whatever day
    for ninety-nine years

because that is what you did.

CALENDAR

Her calendar is full:
today her massage therapist and
   the surgeon who did her hip
tomorrow the acupuncturist
   her hair stylist and
the osteopath
the hypertension specialist the
   cardiologist
then physical therapy
her primary care physician
     and the dentist, overdue
ophthalmologist, optician, otologist and
   the people who fit hearing aids

cleaning ladies on Tuesdays
help in the garden Thursdays
   personal trainer at the gym
the car to the mechanic for that creaky sound
    yoga classes, bridge lessons
the gynecologist, how could she forget the gynecologist
an MRI here, an ultrasound there
   scarcely time to buy groceries

she has no time for friends.

BIRTHDAY PARTY

Not for hip-hop, rap, funk
    not even for YMCA or the Electric Slide

but when it's a foxtrot, a waltz, the Charleston
    especially the Charleston
she lays her hand on her son's shoulder and they dance

She enters her tenth decade
       dancing.

BIGHAT PEOPLE

Bighat people
   you see them everywhere now
   lookalike men and women

clients of Solumbra and Travelsmith
sunshirt sleeves buttoned to the wrist
sunrepellent pants elastic at the cuff
   SPF-30 lotion everywhere

Their beach days are over
   no more shorts bikinis tank tops flip-flops

they don't tan anymore anyway
they spot and freckle
         to their horror they wrinkle

The hard way they've learned
new words: melanoma
                  cutaneous horn
                  basal cell carcinoma

now they are content to stand
                  bighatted
   watching their yellow lab
   bellydeep in pondwater.

SISYPHUS

At first he thinks he'll leave the stone at the summit
    and bring up another one the next day
    build a monument to himself

    or to his work ethic
    a goal to make the whole thing easier

That wasn't what the gods had in mind

He only has one stone
    the same stone
    to push up the hill every day

most days it rolls down
just as he nears the top

other days he coaxes the boulder to the summit
chocks it happily and lies down to rest
wakens to find it and himself back in the valley
    ready for another day
    and another
    and another

It's not the physical labor

the torture is that day
    after toilsome day nothing
is accomplished.

FINISH LINE

For so long the seas have been fair
   a squall here and there
   contrary tides sometimes

one sailor said
   I'm not afraid of dying it's just
   I don't want to miss anything

I always thought the same yet
   on this leg suddenly
   I can see the finish line buoy
my peers lose way
        rudders crack
        spinnakers rip
   frantically they bail
        and try to caulk splitting seams

Their vessels founder
great waves tower over us
        my hull is damaged

as the regatta ends in the rising wind
   I trim sails
   look for the bailing can.

VETERAN

My body is something like
   a veteran of the great war
   remembering itself sunburnt, muscled
   can-do
defender of a noble country
leaning against the ship's rail, grinning
   as its buddy focuses the Kodak

wondering now how it came to be someone else
   ineffectual, limping, no longer answering the call of duty.

PSYCHIC POWERS

When my father and often some of us kids
      arrived on her doorstep
my grandmother always said

I knew you were coming
            I've got a chicken in the oven

My father never told her in advance when we were coming
      he said he didn't want her to go to any trouble
besides, long-distance calls were expensive

I don't remember hugs or kisses or any other greeting
I don't remember sitting at the table, eating the chicken

My brother thought she had psychic powers
He tells of the time he was on a business trip, passing through
      deciding on impulse to stop and say hello
      she met him at the door

I knew you were coming
            I've got a chicken in the oven

I think she cooked a lot of chickens she
      just had to eat, herself.

COULD

I could tell them
   where to find the drinking gourd in the sky

I could tell them apples cure the common cold
   east wind means rain
   the dishwasher is more sanitary than washing by hand
   nine mph over the speed limit is permitted

I could tell them
   they will regret the tattoo
   and the tan

I could say the day will come
   when they will want to know
   who their grandparents were

I could tell them everybody has a story
I could tell them to ask for it
   and to listen

I could tell them mine
   if they wanted to hear it.

BEFORE DRINKING HEMLOCK

Reading Plato
    an adolescent casts the book aside
      disgusted   puzzled
life holds such riches
      success   love   indulgence

Socrates makes no sense

Now
knowing all the crevices of night
    the specters of regret
    the nagging small hours
    the hopeless growing gray

I've come to understand
    sweeter than fame
    sweeter than love
    sweeter than any waking pleasure
is a dreamless night's sleep.

STAND READY

Keats declared himself a poet
    then wrote a few immortal lines
    and many pages of tedium
not understanding that the Muse chooses

the most a mortal can do is volunteer
 and pen in hand
      stand ready.

Acknowledgments

Certain poems in this collection were originally published in *Avalon Literary Review, Brickplight, El Portal, Flights, Freshwater, Lily Poetry Review, Loch Raven Review, Moon City Review, MORIA, Steam Ticket,* and *Triggerfish Critical Review.*

About the Author

Marte Carlock-Clifford is the author of *A Guide to Public Art in Greater Boston*. After almost twenty years of writing for the *Boston Globe,* she decided it's more fun to make things up. She has published articles, short stories, and poems in more than fifty publications. She lives near Boston. This is her second collection of poetry, following *How It Will Be from Now on Out* (Lioncrest, 2023).

www.ingramcontent.com/pod-product-compliance
Lightning Source LLC
Chambersburg PA
CBHW020418130626
46549CB00006B/2625